AFRICAN CRITTERS™

FOREWORD

When I was a boy, I always loved animals and read everything I could find about them. One of my favorite sources of animal information was the *National Geographic* magazine. Each month, *National Geographic's* thrilling photographic stories took me to far-off worlds to meet, and learn to appreciate, animals that were remarkably different from any I would have ever seen in my community. Inspired by my childhood reading and my college studies in environmental science, I have spent my life fighting to save and protect animals. I feel privileged to now run America's largest animal protection organization.

I have never forgotten the important role that National Geographic played in my life, and so I was thrilled to meet and get to know Bobby Haas, a National Geographic photographer whose passion for animals matches my own. It is my hope that his writing and photography in this beautiful book about the wild animals of Africa will inspire you, just as his National Geographic predecessors inspired me. Now, more than ever, the survival of wild animals depends on our defense of their right to live in harmony with people. I hope you'll celebrate the majesty of the animal kingdom and do your best to safeguard all of the wild creatures of the world for their own sake and for the benefit of future generations of children and adults alike.

Wayne Pacelle
President and CEO
The Humane Society of the United States

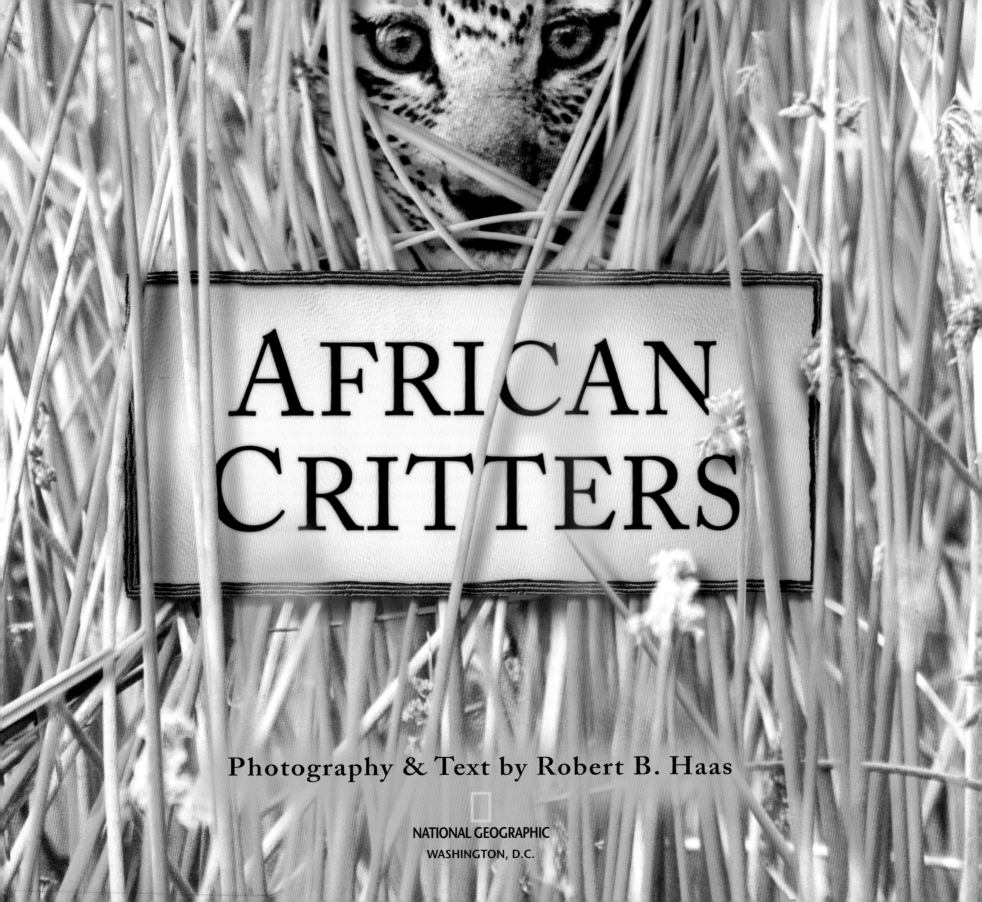

AFRICAN CRITTERS

Photography & Text by Robert B. Haas

NATIONAL GEOGRAPHIC

WASHINGTON, D.C.

This work is dedicated to children…

To every child who has a hero somewhere in the world, whether that hero be Martin Luther King or Angelina Jolie or Tiger Woods. Your heroes are famous or entertaining or exceptional in some way. But for those few of you who cannot bear the thought of a world without cheetahs or tigers or wild dogs, you too can reach the lofty heights of stardom. If you play a role in saving an endangered species, you will have changed the world…and you will be a hero of the planet.

And to my children Samantha, Courtney and Vanessa—You are my heroes.

Published by the National Geographic Society, 1145 17th Street N.W., Washington, D.C. 20036-4688.
All rights reserved. Reproduction of the whole or any part of the contents without written permission from the publisher is prohibited.

Book design by Cosgrove Associates, Inc., and revision updates by Lisa Lytton.

Library of Congress Cataloging-in-Publication Information is available from the Library of Congress upon request.
ISBN: 978-1-4263-0317-3 (hardcover)
ISBN: 978-1-4263-0318-0 (reinforced library binding)

For information about special discounts for bulk purchases, please contact
National Geographic Books Special Sales: ngspecsales@ngs.org
For rights or permissions inquiries, please contact
National Geographic Books Subsidiary Rights: ngbookrights@ngs.org

Kids and parents, please visit us at: www.nationalgeographic.com/books
Librarians and teachers, please visit us at: www.ngchildrensbooks.com

Printed in China

CONTENTS

MY TYPICAL DAY

5-6 am – Wake up, have toast and coffee, load up the jeep

6-11 am – Find and photograph animals on a morning game drive

11-Noon – Eat a huge breakfast in camp

Noon-2 pm – Rest and read

2-3 pm – Snack of cheese and fruit

3-6 pm – Afternoon game drive

6-7 pm – Shower and change clothes

7-9 pm – Dinner and talk about our game drives

9 pm – Lights out! It's been a long day

WELCOME TO AFRICA

AFRICA

I went on my first safari when I was 47 years old. I already loved animals. The wonderful pack of dogs that live with my family taught me that. But when I first saw the brilliant black and white stripes of a zebra and the blinding speed of a sprinting cheetah, that love of animals rose to a new level.

There is something magical about watching wild animals in their natural surroundings. It is a step back in time. There are no buildings, no wars, and no clocks to disturb their daily routines. We are able to witness scenes that took place tens of thousands of years ago.

I have photographed critters in South Africa, Botswana, Kenya, and Namibia. But wherever I go, I have one routine. When I first arrive in camp, I talk to my guide to find out what animals have been spotted recently and where. Then every morning I go out with the guide in a jeep with an open top. I carry binoculars to spot critters and a few different cameras and lenses to take photo-graphs. I start my day very early, at about 6:00 **a.m.**, and stop taking pictures in the late afternoon or early evening. The early morning sunlight and the soft light from a setting sun are often best for taking beauti-ful photographs. In the middle of the day, I have lunch and rest for a few hours. This is a good time for a break because the critters are resting, too. They usually nap in the shade to escape the mid-day heat. In the evening, I have a chance to share my day with other travelers and photographers who are staying at the same camp.

In *African Critters*, you will see my photo-graphs and read stories about my adventures in Africa. These stories are completely true. That is the beauty of animals. There is nothing to be gained by making up stories—the real ones are the best.

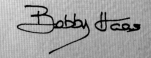

THE LEOPARDS
OF SINGITA

The leopard is a mysterious critter.

It hunts mostly at night, so people rarely get to see it. If you look carefully, you might catch a glimpse of a leopard lying asleep in a tree, hidden behind thick leaves and branches. But usually that's the closest you can get to a leopard.

"The Leopards of Singita" is the story of a mother leopard and two leopard cubs that my guide and I found hidden in a small cave in the African wilderness.

On our first afternoon at Singita, a game reserve in South Africa, we unpacked our gear at the camp and then decided to look for two newborn leopard cubs we had heard about.

The cubs were not in the den where they were born. No one staying at the camp had seen them for a week or two. We knew that the mother had hidden her young critters in a very safe spot.

It was late afternoon by the time we set out. We drove slowly in the direction of the old den. Even though the mother had abandoned this site, we thought the new den might not be too far away.

LEARNING ABOUT LEOPARDS

The leopard is a predator (a hunter) that almost always searches for its prey (animals to kill for food) at night. Since so few leopards are seen during the day, it is surprising to learn that there are about 100,000 leopards roaming the African wilderness. Actually, there are more leopards in Africa than lions and cheetahs combined.

Just before sunset, we reached the bank of a river. We were sitting in our jeep peering through binoculars when I saw a tiny spotted head poke out of a small cave and growl. It was one of the leopard cubs. We had found the new den.

We were on the opposite side of the river, about 50 yards away from the cubs. But we decided not to get any closer. We didn't want to scare them away. So we just waited. And then it happened. First one cub and then the other crawled out of the cave and onto the nearby rocks. We took lots and lots of pictures.

In a few minutes, the sun dipped below the hills, and our photo session was over.

Very early the next morning,
we set off in search of the mother.

We knew that our best photos would come only after she returned to the den and the cubs could play under her watchful eye.

We finally spotted her far from her den on the bough of a marula tree, pacing back and forth. Within a few seconds, she jumped from one bough to another and scampered down the tree.

The leopard silently strode through the tall grass, hidden from its prey. Suddenly, she leaped in a graceful arc and landed on a small African hare.

LEARNING ABOUT LEOPARDS

Even though the leopard is smaller than a lion, it has a unique talent that allows it to enjoy a fresh meal without fear of other critters. The leopard has the ability to leap up a tall tree carrying even a full-grown antelope in its jaws. It will then cache (hide) the carcass in the tree and feed over the next day or two in peace and quiet.

After eating the hare, the mother began the long, slow journey back to the den site. When she arrived at the edge of the river, her cubs ran out of the tiny cave and greeted her with bouncing leaps and licking tongues.

Every once in a while, the mother growled in our direction. But she let my camera capture shots of the cubs playing on the rocks, climbing trees, wrestling in the grass, and even drinking her milk.

In the early afternoon, the exhausted cubs fell asleep. The mother climbed a nearby tree and snoozed too. We had been very lucky. We had watched one of Africa's most magnificent critters, both as a deadly hunter and as a tender and loving parent.

THE ELEPHANTS
OF OKAVANGO

Each critter in Africa begins life as part of a family. Some, like the leopard cubs, live alone with their mother. Others, including elephant babies, live in a herd, or large group, that includes their own family and others as well. Elephants are usually very peaceful, but the herd will fiercely defend a baby elephant in danger.

Deep in the heart of the Okavango region of Botswana, we climbed out of our jeep to take photos of a green chameleon in the road. All of a sudden, we heard the earsplitting sound of an elephant's roar. Inside the forest, only 30 yards away, stood a young male elephant staring right at us! Slowly, we climbed back into our jeep. But the young bull raised his trunk and charged toward us, shaking his head back and forth. Only when the angry elephant stopped in his tracks did we realize that this was only a warning, or "false charge." Our hearts were beating very fast, and it took a while for us to calm down. An elephant, even a young one, is a dangerous animal!

LEARNING ABOUT ELEPHANTS

The Okavango region is an enormous wilderness area that covers a large portion of the country of Botswana in southern Africa. It is almost the same size as the state of Connecticut. In the months of August and September each year, large herds of elephants roam across the Okavango along the banks of its rivers.

After we drove away, we photographed zebras and impalas grazing on the savanna. But we were not relaxed for long. Suddenly another elephant charged out of the forest right for our jeep! And it was no false charge this time.

My guide held out his hand and shouted "Whoa!"

I could not believe my ears! A charging elephant and our only defense was an outstretched arm! But sure enough, the elephant stopped in its tracks.

By this time, we figured that the entire herd must be in a terrible mood. Normally, elephants are calm so long as you don't threaten their babies. We wondered what was causing this strange behavior.

LEARNING ABOUT ELEPHANTS

Young elephant bulls tend to wander on their own, away from the herd, once they become teenagers. The bulls return to the herd occasionally, but usually for only short amounts of time. When there are no older female elephants around, the young bulls are aggressive and rowdy with each other, often fighting and testing their strength. Bulls are most aggressive during short periods called "musth," when their glands are swollen and they are interested in mating with females.

Even the smallest members of the herd were acting aggressive. Two very young elephants approached our jeep and raised their trunks straight up in the air.

At last we discovered what was going on. Inside a group of about 20 elephants, we spotted the newest member of the herd—a *tiny* baby no larger than an antelope. This little critter must have been only a few days old!

We watched for a long time and were amazed at how the baby could keep up with the herd and not be crushed by the enormous legs of the elephants who formed a tight circle around him.

LEARNING ABOUT ELEPHANTS

Elephant herds vary in size, but the larger ones have 15 to 20 members or more. The herd is usually made up of mother elephants and their children. Since older males only join the group occasionally, the herd is almost always led by the largest female, who is called the "matriarch." The females in the herd stay close to each other and are very careful to protect the infants from any type of threat.

LEARNING ABOUT ELEPHANTS

Even though full-grown elephants weigh five tons (5,000 kg), elephants share many traits with humans. Elephants are known to live 60 years or more. The members of a herd communicate with each other regularly through low rumbling sounds, loud growls, trumpeting and squeals that express many different emotions. At the death of a member of the herd, elephants are clearly disturbed, showing feelings that closely resemble sadness in humans.

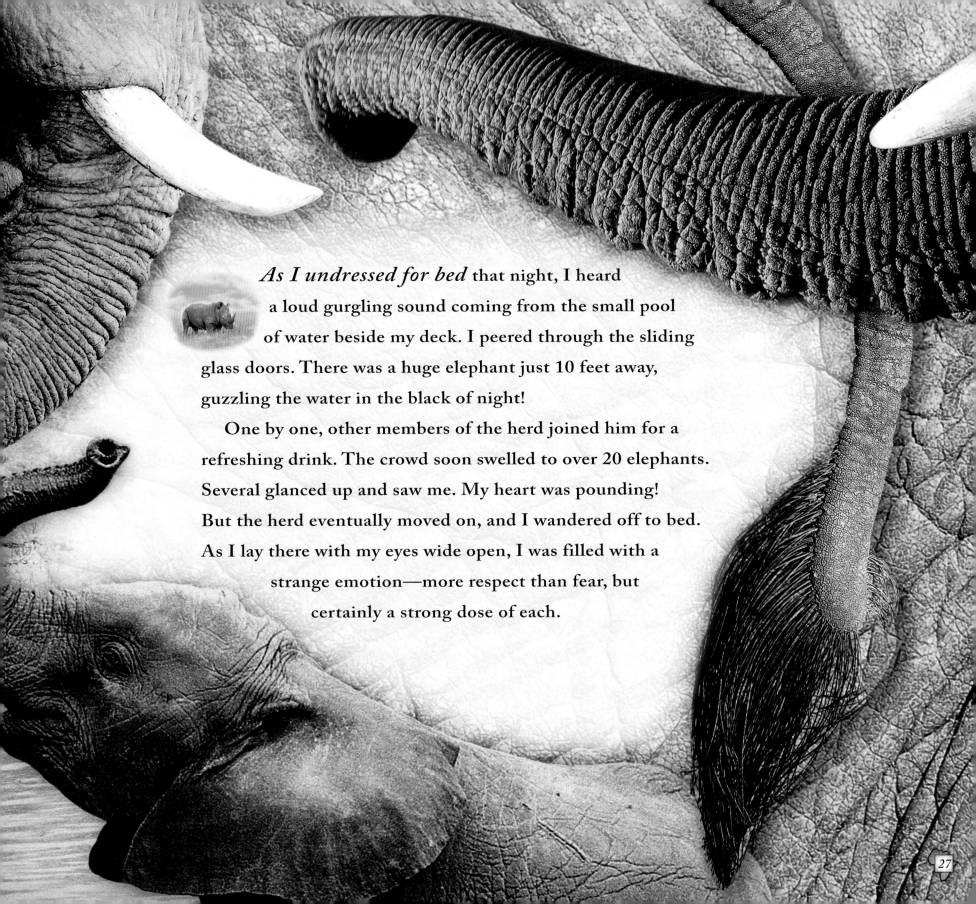

As I undressed for bed that night, I heard
a loud gurgling sound coming from the small pool
of water beside my deck. I peered through the sliding
glass doors. There was a huge elephant just 10 feet away,
guzzling the water in the black of night!

One by one, other members of the herd joined him for a
refreshing drink. The crowd soon swelled to over 20 elephants.
Several glanced up and saw me. My heart was pounding!
But the herd eventually moved on, and I wandered off to bed.
As I lay there with my eyes wide open, I was filled with a
strange emotion—more respect than fear, but
certainly a strong dose of each.

THE WILD DOGS
OF MALA MALA

We got our first glimpse of a pack of wild dogs in the open grasslands of Mala Mala Camp in South Africa. We knew this was a rare sighting—about 15 wild dogs of all sizes frolicking in the late afternoon. Each member of the pack had a different pattern of patches on its coat. Their faces were so dark that it was almost impossible to see their golden eyes behind their black muzzles.

The wild dogs were no larger than small German shepherds. They did not look very strong. Their legs were thin and long, and their enormous ears looked way too big for their heads. But soon we learned why the wild dog is considered such a great hunter.

Suddenly the pack was perfectly still. Even the puppies stopped their yapping and sat rigid in the grass. We did not make a sound in our jeep.

LEARNING ABOUT WILD DOGS

The wild dog is one of Africa's most endangered critters, with only about 3,000 to 5,000 still roaming free. Wild dogs are often attacked and killed by lions, who chase the pack away from a carcass of fresh meat. But the wild dog's worst enemy is people. For many years, hunters shot wild dogs for sport or simply to eliminate a critter that was considered a pest.

A small herd of impalas was grazing in the distance. As the impalas slowly moved in the direction of the wild dogs, the closest members of the dog pack crouched in the stalking position with their heads and necks extended and their bright-colored tails down between their legs.

We could almost sense what the dogs were thinking. They were waiting for the impalas to come a bit closer, but they knew that if they waited too long and their prey spotted them, they would lose their chance for a meal.

LEARNING ABOUT WILD DOGS

The wild dog is a nomadic critter, one that wanders around very large territories in search of prey. Unlike lions or leopards, a pack of wild dogs needs a huge area of land in order to survive. It must avoid its enemies, such as lions, as it hunts and raises its young. And people must be willing to allow the wild dog to exist inside large wilderness reserves, where animals are protected from hunters.

We could feel the tension mount as the impalas grazed closer. One wild dog inched forward in the grass with the other dogs right behind. Suddenly, the pack exploded in a rush toward the impala herd.

Within seconds, the impalas spotted the pack. They split into three groups, which took off in different directions. Acting as if this had all been planned in advance, the wild dog pack also split into three groups, each one chasing after one of the impala groups. All the critters disappeared, dashing into the forest.

For a few minutes there was complete silence. Then we heard excited barking. We knew the hunt was over.

As we drove around, we found that each group of dogs had brought down one impala. As we caught our breath, we were filled with both admiration for the wild dogs and sympathy for the impalas. We could see now where wild dogs got their reputation for fierceness!

Then we noticed two wild dogs who had not been part of the hunt limping over to one of the impala kills. One was dragging a broken rear leg, and the other had deep wounds around its back and belly that looked like they were made by a trap. The pack let the injured dogs eat as much as they wanted. Some dogs carried scraps of food to the hungry puppies.

Watching and photographing, we gained great respect for wild dogs. They might be fierce hunters, but they care for members of the pack who can't care for themselves.

THE LIONS
OF SABI SAND

Beneath the surface of African rivers, the powerful crocodile rules a watery kingdom. In the skies above, the mighty martial eagle, with wings as wide as a man is tall, reigns supreme. And on land, only one animal can claim the crown as the King of Beasts—the African lion.

LEARNING ABOUT LIONS

Lions are not the largest critters in all of Africa. Giraffes are far taller, hippos and rhinos weigh more than four or five lions combined, and an elephant has more strength in its trunk alone than a lion has in its entire body. But the lion is by far the largest predator in Africa, with powerful claws that can tear through the hide of a zebra. And lions often hunt in packs of five or more.

As soon as we arrived in the Sabi Sand region of South Africa, we drove our jeep in search of a mother lioness who had given birth to baby cubs just three months before. The first thing she did when she saw us was to roar very loudly. She had given us a stern warning to stay away. We waited patiently until the mother lioness calmed down and let us get closer. We were thrilled to see that she had triplets! The youngsters were guarded by both the lioness and a huge father lion. The three frisky cubs wrestled in the tall grass, climbed trees, and tugged at Mom's ears with tiny, sharp teeth.

The lioness went hunting for several hours that day and later walked back to the cubs with the body of a small antelope in her jaws. The lioness dropped the food in front of the curious youngsters, but they just stared at it. Maybe this was their first meal of fresh meat. At last, the mother lioness took a bite, and the cubs learned what to do at the dinner table.

After a meal of fresh antelope and warm mother's milk, the cubs snuggled together for a long nap. And we drove off in search of other critters.

We drove our jeep right up to a herd of more than 100 buffaloes! A few of them were so close that we could have touched their hides! But we didn't. Instead, we moved very cautiously—a buffalo is a dangerous brute.

LEARNING ABOUT LIONS

A single group of lions, called a "pride," may lose many cubs to starvation, disease, or predators before even a single cub survives! After a few months, cubs need to eat more than just mother's milk. The mother must bring back fresh meat from her hunting every few days. And to do that, she sometimes has to leave them alone—and in danger—for hours at a time.

Early the next morning, we returned to the lion's hiding place, or lair. In the middle of the night, the adult lions had captured a giraffe and dragged it back for a feast that would last for days.

After a hearty meal, the father lion lay down for a nap, resting his head on the giraffe as if it were a nice, soft pillow. The lioness thought that this would be a good time for her to snack on the giraffe. Disturbed, the lion woke up and charged the lioness. But she didn't back down—she growled at the lion and swung her claws at his nose.

LEARNING ABOUT LIONS

A pride of lions does not share a meal like one big happy family. Usually, the male lions take their share first before the female lionesses eat. If there is any meat left after the adults have finished, the young cubs take their turn last.

LEARNING ABOUT LIONS

The buffalo and the lion are deadly enemies. Lions will attack a buffalo for the meat that it provides. And a buffalo, with its great strength and sharp horns, will fight back ferociously. It is a battle of titans in which either one can die.

After a morning watching hungry lions, we drove our jeep into the shade for a picnic lunch of egg salad sandwiches and fresh fruit. After we ate, we closed our eyes for a short nap. But then my guide got a message over his walkie-talkie from another guide in a different safari jeep—buffaloes were trying to kill the lion cubs!

The herd of buffaloes had found the cubs lying in the grass when the adult lions were away hunting. The buffaloes had tried to crush the tiny cubs, knowing that the cubs were children of their enemy.

When we got to the scene of the buffalo attack, there was tension in the air! The herd was still wandering around in a nasty mood. We spotted the dead body of one of the three cubs, lying in the grass.

Then we spotted a second cub hiding under a small bush—alive! The terrified cub was breathing hard with its eyes wide open. We worried it might be badly injured. We couldn't find the third cub anywhere. Luckily, the buffaloes couldn't find either cub and walked away.

When it was dark, we headed back to camp. There was nothing we could do—only the lioness could save her children. Deadly battles and narrow escapes are part of nature's way.

Early the next morning, we drove back to the scene of the attack. The cub we thought might be injured was gone! Either the cub had been found by a predator or the mother had rescued him. There was no trace of the third cub. We went straight to the lion's lair. We could not believe our eyes! The cub we had last seen hiding alone under a bush was lying in the grass. He was tired and whimpering but still alive. And the third cub was sitting with its mother, safe and sound.

THE SCAVENGERS
OF THE SAVANNA

In the animal world, it is wrong to pin the label of "good guys" on certain critters and "bad guys" on other critters. Each type of animal must survive in its own way.

For most meat-eaters, or carnivores, finding food is difficult and dangerous. It means capturing other critters who are usually able to escape and often willing to fight for their lives.

Certain critters, known as "scavengers," will feed on the meat and bones left behind by other hunters. The best-known scavenger in all of Africa is the hyena.

After many safaris I had learned to respect the hyena as an animal with unique skills and a special role in the African wilderness. At first, I thought the hyena was simply a scavenger who would eat scraps from a fresh lion kill. But the hyena is also a fierce hunter who brings down prey after a chase that lasts for miles. And hyenas play an important role in their ecosystem. With a huge set of powerful jaws, they crush and eat even the largest bones left behind by lions and leopards. That way, they recycle food that others can't digest.

LEARNING ABOUT HYENAS

African meat-eaters cannot be neatly divided into predators who hunt for their own meals and scavengers who feed on leftovers. Scavengers such as hyenas and jackals are also skillful hunters. And even the most powerful predators, such as lions and leopards, will "borrow" dinner by chasing a cheetah away from its hard-earned kill.

Over the years I had learned a great deal about the habits of the hyena. But I'd never photographed tiny hyena cubs until I was on safari at Londolozi Camp in South Africa.

My guide and I heard at the camp that there was a new litter of spotted hyena cubs just a month or two old, but no one had seen the cubs in a while. From time to time, hyena mothers will abandon one den site and set up another to hide the cubs from attack by lions.

At the first den site, there was no trace of any cubs. Less than a mile away, we came across an adult hyena lying beside a huge termite mound. We watched quietly, and one by one, a pair of hyena cubs climbed out from underneath the mound and squinted their eyes in the bright sunlight.

LEARNING ABOUT HYENAS

The largest type of hyena in Africa is known as the spotted hyena. Spotted hyena cubs are all black. The coat of an adult is thick and coarse with dark spots, and its muzzle is black. Female spotted hyenas are larger than males, and the clan is usually led by a female. Even though clan members often hunt as a team, once their prey is brought down, each hyena fights for its share of the carcass.

For the next hour or so, we took pictures as the cubs explored the den site. They sniffed the grass, then climbed on their mother's back and chewed her ears. With thick black coats and round bellies, the cubs were like a pair of puppies. Many baby critters behave this way. Their world is filled with play and love, and their tummies are filled with Mother's milk.

After a while, the mother hyena closed her eyes for a short nap, and the tired cubs snuggled up against her thick fur.

59

All of a sudden the mother raised her head, perked up her ears, and sprang into action. She lifted one of the cubs in her jaws and carried it into the den under the termite mound. Then she picked up the second cub. We followed her for a mile or so to an old den site. She dropped the cub there, then scampered back to get the other. In less than 20 minutes, the mother had sensed danger and switched dens.

A few weeks later, a lion discovered the new den site and killed the hyena cubs. Lions and hyenas destroy each other's cubs to protect their hunting territory from competitors. Even though this is all part of the natural life-and-death struggle in Africa, I still felt sad about the loss of the young hyenas.

THE BIG GRAYS

Hippos and rhinos, the "big grays" of Africa, are not the most popular animals to photograph. They don't leap up trees like leopards or run like cheetahs or stalk like lions. But the big grays have a mystical quality and a timeless beauty. These critters walked the Earth and soaked in its waters for millions of years before humans arrived on the scene.

 *There are many* similarities between hippos and rhinos. They are both very heavy. A full-grown male hippo weighs between 3,000 and 6,000 pounds, while a male rhino tips the scales at 2,000 to 4,500 pounds. Their hides are quite thick and gray in color, and both critters are grazers, animals who feed on grass and other plants.

But there are differences as well. A rhino has a large horn at the end of its snout, and a hippo doesn't. Rhinos spend most of their time on land but enjoy a mud bath in a shallow pool. Hippos soak all day in rivers and lakes but come out of the water to feed at night.

LEARNING ABOUT RHINOS

The rhinoceros uses its horn to fight off predators and to do battle with other rhinos. But the rhino's horn has also been its worst enemy. Poachers (illegal hunters) will kill rhinos just for their horns. The poacher then sells the horn as a souvenir or to people who believe that crushed rhinoceros horn is a powerful medicine.

LEARNING ABOUT HIPPOS

In the water, hippopotamuses bunch together in large clusters. Baby hippos drink their mother's milk underwater. On land, each adult hippo grazes by itself. Young hippos feed with their mothers. If a young hippo wanders away from its mother on land, Mom will punish the youngster by bumping or even gently biting its hide.

Adult hippos and rhinos have very little to fear from any other critter. And they fiercely protect their young. An angry hippo's huge jaws are strong enough to cut a crocodile in half, making a baby hippo a pretty risky crocodile dinner! On land, rhino mothers fight off lions and hyenas that might attack their young.

For many years, humans have been the greatest threat to rhinos. In the past, hunters killed so many rhinos that they almost became extinct in the wild. But today, the hunting of rhinos is forbidden almost everywhere in Africa, and the rhino population is on the rise.

Both rhinos and hippos are suspicious of people and very territorial. If their territory is invaded, the big grays are fast runners. I should know. I was charged twice by an angry hippo, once in Kenya when I crawled too close to a stream where it was bathing and once in Namibia when I was taking pictures from a very small boat. And I was charged by a rhino when we stopped our safari jeep too close to its midden, the pile of droppings that it was using to mark the boundaries of its territory.

The big grays are magnificent creatures …but we all must respect their right to live without being disturbed by humans.

ITTY BITTY CRITTERS

Beauty comes in all shapes and sizes in the wilds of Africa, and often the largest and smallest critters live side by side in perfect harmony. "Itty Bitty Critters" explores some of the fascinating stories and lifestyles that exist at the micro level in Africa.

The oxpecker is a tiny bird with a bright red beak. It enjoys a special relationship with the largest critters in Africa, especially the buffalo. Oxpeckers often travel with a herd of buffaloes. They bounce all around the buffalo's hide, inside its ears, and even up its nose in search of tiny insects to feed on.

It is an unusual relationship that works just fine for both critters—the oxpecker enjoys a tasty meal at its favorite "restaurant," and the buffalo gets rid of an annoying itch.

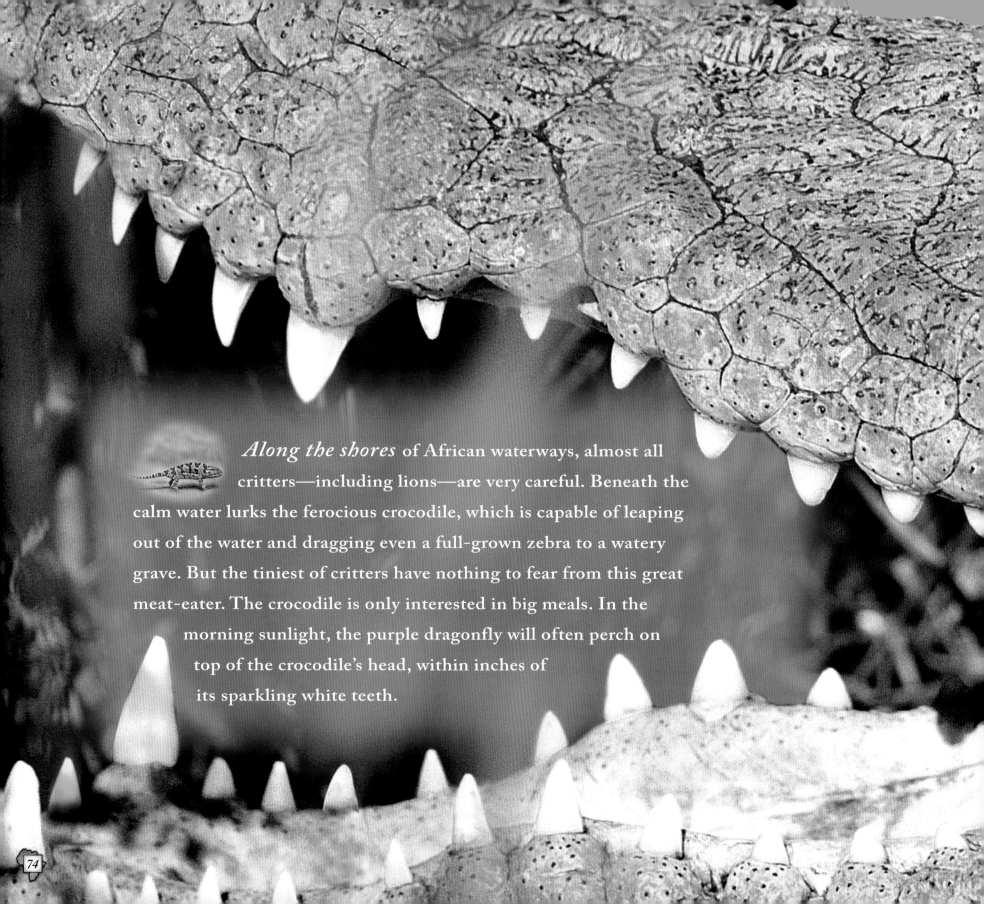

Along the shores of African waterways, almost all critters—including lions—are very careful. Beneath the calm water lurks the ferocious crocodile, which is capable of leaping out of the water and dragging even a full-grown zebra to a watery grave. But the tiniest of critters have nothing to fear from this great meat-eater. The crocodile is only interested in big meals. In the morning sunlight, the purple dragonfly will often perch on top of the crocodile's head, within inches of its sparkling white teeth.

In the African wilderness, nothing goes to waste. Even elephant droppings the size of softballs have a special use. The male dung beetle inspects a pile of droppings and selects one. It then works furiously to shape the dropping into a round ball.

With back legs up against the dung ball and front legs on the ground, the dung beetle moves backward on its two front legs pushing the ball into the bushes. It then offers the dung ball to a female dung beetle. If the female is impressed, she will accept this gift and lay a single egg in the dung ball. The egg hatches after a week, and the life of a new dung beetle begins.

THE CHEETAHS
OF PHINDA

The open grassland of Africa is home to a fantastic variety of critters, and each critter has its own special traits. The cheetah's most famous trait is speed.

There is no animal alive today that can match the speed of the cheetah. When a cheetah chases after an antelope, it seems to fly across the savanna. But sometimes, speed alone cannot save the cheetah from its enemies.

We had just arrived at a South African wildlife camp called Phinda, which is famous for cheetahs. As soon as we unpacked, we drove out into the savanna in our jeep, ready to take photos. The rainy season had just ended, and the grass was very tall. It would not be easy to spot a cheetah lying down. We searched all over Phinda for hours and saw many other critters, but not even one cheetah! We were tired and disappointed when we returned to camp that night.

LEARNING ABOUT CHEETAHS

There are only a few thousand cheetahs in all of Africa. And the ones who are still left will hide to avoid both poachers and larger animals. Since the few cheetahs that do live in the wild are so cautious, it can be hard for a photographer to find them.

The first hour or two after sunrise is the perfect time to find cheetahs. They are often on the prowl hunting for breakfast in the cool morning air. Early the next morning, we found two full-grown cheetah brothers very close to our camp. Lying in the tall grass, the brothers spotted a small antelope, and the chase was on!

The antelope raced into a thicket of bushes with the speedy cheetahs right on its tail. Inside the thicket, the cheetahs lost the antelope. The clever critter had dashed safely out the other side of the bushes. The chase was over. The cheetahs walked away with empty stomachs. Finding a meal in the wild is not like going to the grocery store.

LEARNING ABOUT CHEETAHS

The animals I photographed in Africa are wild and free.
A lion will attack a cheetah to take its food away. Lions,
leopards, and hyenas kill cheetah cubs so that the cubs do
not grow up and hunt the same animals they do. There is
always danger in the air.

On our third day at Phinda, we found the cheetah brothers walking single file, ready to hunt.

Then we noticed a mother cheetah and her four one-year-old cubs crouched in the grass. The cheetah family was afraid of the brothers! A grown male cheetah will attack other cheetahs to protect his hunting territory. Luckily, the brothers did not see them.

For the rest of the day, we photographed the cubs. A mother cheetah has a very difficult job raising cubs on her own. When she hunts, she hides her cubs from lions or leopards who could hurt them. And she must be a great hunter to feed her family. This remarkable mother had kept all four cubs alive for a whole year.

LEARNING ABOUT CHEETAHS

When they are almost two years old, young cheetahs leave their mother to begin life on their own. The male cubs stay together, but the female cubs soon move away to start their own families. After mating with a female cheetah, a male cheetah leaves the female to raise the cubs on her own. Cheetah brothers often hunt together, play together, and sleep together for the rest of their lives.

Very early on the morning of our fourth day at Phinda, we spotted the cheetah family in a nearby thicket. But we saw only the four cubs—the mother was missing! The frightened cubs were calling their mother with a loud chirping noise. We were worried. If their mother had been killed, the four cubs would probably not survive on their own.

Then we heard a soft cheetah chirp from nearby bushes. It was the mother cheetah! She had been trapped by the two cheetah brothers and was snarling and hissing at them. The brothers wanted to mate with her and have a new litter of baby cheetahs. But she was not ready for another family—her young cubs still needed all her attention.

LEARNING ABOUT CHEETAHS

Chirping is one of many different sounds that cheetahs use to talk to each other in the wild. An angry cheetah will snarl or cough. A mother cheetah will make a purring sound like a cat to tell her cubs to follow her. And cheetah cubs who are fighting over a meal will squeal like pigs.

The confused cubs stared at each other wondering what to do.
Then, led by one brave little cheetah, the cubs marched into the
bushes and stood by their mother's side. Suddenly, the brothers
growled and rushed at the cubs! The terrified cubs dashed out of the
bushes. All except one. The cub closest to his mother did not budge.
Would the brothers attack this brave cub or let him live?

For a few scary moments, no one moved. Finally, the cheetah
brothers allowed the cub to snuggle with his mother.
Soon, the other cubs returned, and all seven cheetahs—
including the brothers—curled up together for a nap
in the cool shade.

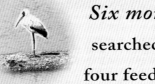 *Six months later,* we returned to Phinda and searched for the cheetah cubs. We found three of the four feeding on a huge antelope. It must have been a ferocious fight! The antelope was almost as large as the three cheetahs put together, and it would have attacked them with its sharp horns and kicking hooves. But the mother had taught her cubs well.

At the end of the safari, we still had not seen the fourth cub. Africa is a land of many mysteries, and what happened to that cub was one of its secrets.

CAST OF CRITTERS

Antelope — A wide variety of antelopes roams the African plains, from the tiny 11-pound (5 kilogram) dik-dik to the 250-pound (115 kilogram) male nyala. Their behavior is often very unusual – the gerenuk feeds standing up on its hind legs, and the springbok pronks—leaps in the air—at the sight of a predator.

Buffalo — Weighing up to 1,500 pounds (almost 700 kilograms), the African buffalo travels in herds that range in size from just a few to more than one thousand members. In order to protect themselves, a group of buffaloes will often band together to resist a lion attack.

Cheetah — Even with its long, thin legs, a cheetah stands less than three feet tall at the top of its shoulder. No other animal on land is able to match the speed of a cheetah, which can sprint at over 60 miles (100 kilometers) per hour.

Crocodile — With incredible speed and powerful jaws, a crocodile is able to capture even a zebra drinking at the water's edge. Crocodiles and their American relative, the alligator, have survived from the time of dinosaurs over 65 million years ago.

Dung Beetle — A tiny African dung beetle depends on the massive elephant for almost all its needs. Elephant droppings provide food for the dung beetle, a nest for its unhatched eggs, and, once the newborn beetle emerges from the egg, food for the young, as well.

Eagle — Africa is home to a variety of birds of prey that hunt small animals on land or fish just below the surface of the water. The martial eagle is one of the largest birds of prey, with incredibly strong eyesight to spot its target and sharp talons, or claws, to carry away its meal.

Elephant — The largest land animal of all, the African elephant may grow to a height of more than 10 feet (3 meters) and a weight of over 12,000 pounds (5,500 kilograms). The elephant's trunk is an enormously versatile tool. The elephant uses it to suck up water to

Warthog

Dragonfly

Baboon

Serval Cat

Beetle

Nyala

Butterfly

Tortoise

Vulture

Secretary Bird

drink, rip away grass to eat, express affection with a gentle touch, sniff out smells over a large area, and signal danger to the herd with a loud trumpeting sound.

Giraffe — With a long and graceful neck, the giraffe is taller than any other animal alive, at a height of up to 18 feet (5.5 meters). Despite its gentle appearance, the giraffe is able to protect itself in the African wilds. One kick from its powerful front legs can injure or even kill an attacking lion.

Hippopotamus — The hippopotamus, hippo for short, is truly an amphibious animal—one that spends time both on land and under water. Despite its huge bulk, the hippo moves rapidly through the water in order to chase away any intruder within its territory.

Hyena — With long legs in front and short legs in back, the hyena's body slopes downward. The large spotted hyena lives in many different habitats, from open savanna to thick woodlands, and is one of Africa's most numerous large carnivores, or meat-eaters.

Impala — The impala is a type of antelope that weighs about as much as a full-grown cheetah. Since impalas in southern Africa all mate at nearly the same time, all baby impalas born each year are born within just a few weeks of one another.

Leopard — The leopard is usually smaller than the spotted hyena and weighs about the same as a cheetah. Although leopards are normally very protective of their territory, a mother leopard is willing to share her territory and meals with a full-grown youngster who has recently left her care.

Lion — Even though the male lion weighs almost twice as much as the female, the lion hunting party is often made up of only females. In a pride—a group of lions—the females are usually all related to one another.

Rhinoceros — Africa is home to two different types of rhinoceros. They are called the white rhino and the black rhino even though both species are gray. The larger and less aggressive white rhino has a wide and square mouth, while the black rhino is more aggressive and has a pointed mouth.

Wild Dogs — In each pack of wild dogs, there is only one pair of adults that breeds new puppies. But once the puppies are born, the other members of the pack assist in their care and feeding.

Zebra — The African zebra shares many traits with the North American horse. In the wild, males fight over who will be the leader of the herd, and pairs of zebras rub each other with their heads just as horses do.

Vervet Monkey

Oryx

Millipede

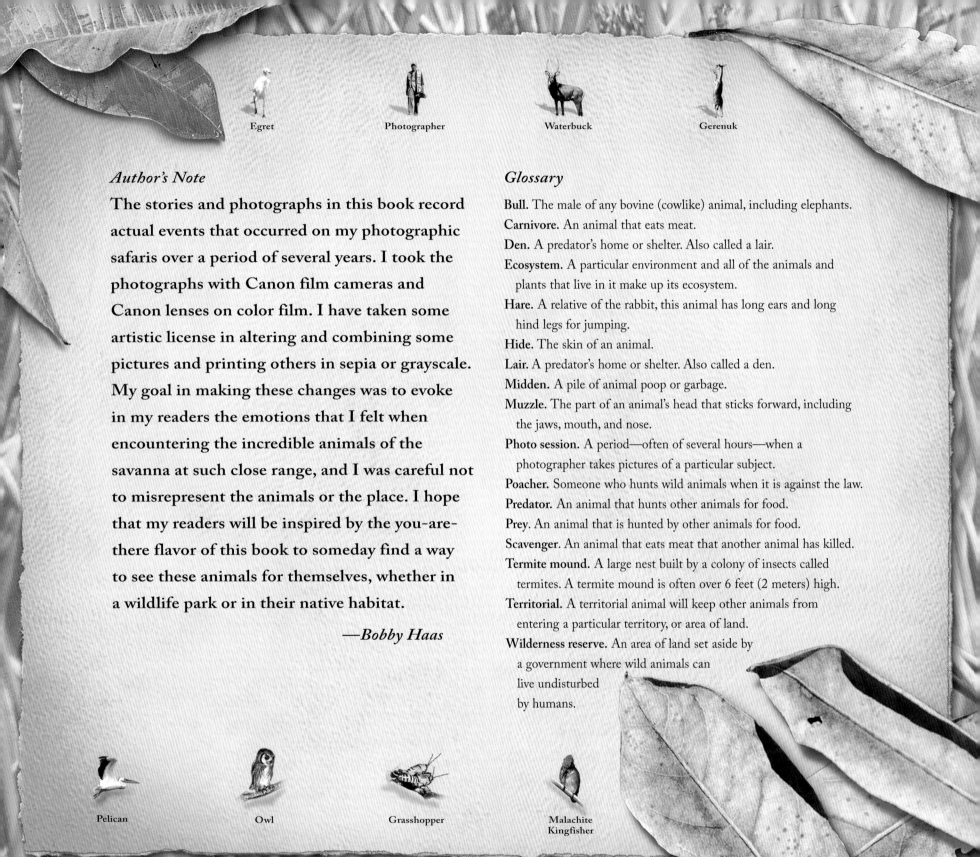

Egret

Photographer

Waterbuck

Gerenuk

Author's Note

The stories and photographs in this book record actual events that occurred on my photographic safaris over a period of several years. I took the photographs with Canon film cameras and Canon lenses on color film. I have taken some artistic license in altering and combining some pictures and printing others in sepia or grayscale. My goal in making these changes was to evoke in my readers the emotions that I felt when encountering the incredible animals of the savanna at such close range, and I was careful not to misrepresent the animals or the place. I hope that my readers will be inspired by the you-are-there flavor of this book to someday find a way to see these animals for themselves, whether in a wildlife park or in their native habitat.

—*Bobby Haas*

Glossary

Bull. The male of any bovine (cowlike) animal, including elephants.

Carnivore. An animal that eats meat.

Den. A predator's home or shelter. Also called a lair.

Ecosystem. A particular environment and all of the animals and plants that live in it make up its ecosystem.

Hare. A relative of the rabbit, this animal has long ears and long hind legs for jumping.

Hide. The skin of an animal.

Lair. A predator's home or shelter. Also called a den.

Midden. A pile of animal poop or garbage.

Muzzle. The part of an animal's head that sticks forward, including the jaws, mouth, and nose.

Photo session. A period—often of several hours—when a photographer takes pictures of a particular subject.

Poacher. Someone who hunts wild animals when it is against the law.

Predator. An animal that hunts other animals for food.

Prey. An animal that is hunted by other animals for food.

Scavenger. An animal that eats meat that another animal has killed.

Termite mound. A large nest built by a colony of insects called termites. A termite mound is often over 6 feet (2 meters) high.

Territorial. A territorial animal will keep other animals from entering a particular territory, or area of land.

Wilderness reserve. An area of land set aside by a government where wild animals can live undisturbed by humans.

Pelican

Owl

Grasshopper

Malachite Kingfisher

Starling

Butterfly

Ostrich

Lilacbreasted Roller

Index

Numbers in **boldface** refer to pictures.

References

This book is a memoir of my own experiences, so I needed no reference for the stories themselves. For information on the animals for the text, fact boxes, and Cast of Critters, I consulted the reference sources below.

Burnie, David, and Don E. Wilson. *Animal.* New York: DK Publishing, Inc., and Smithsonian Institution, 2001.

Estes, Richard D. *The Behavior Guide to African Mammals.* Los Angeles: University of California Press, 1991.

Sinclair, Ian, Phil Hockey and Warwick Tarboton. *Birds of Southern Africa.* Cape Town, South Africa: Struik Publishers, 1993.

More Books From National Geographic Photographers

If you want to find out more about National Geographic photographers and how they work with animals, check out the *Face to Face with Animals* series:

Face to Face with Caterpillars
by Darlyne A. Murawski

Face to Face with Cheetahs
by Chris Johns

Face to Face with Dolphins
by Flip and Linda Nicklin

Face to Face with Elephants
by Beverly and Dereck Joubert

Face to Face with Frogs
by Mark Moffett

Face to Face with Grizzlies
by Joel Sartore

Face to Face with Lions
by Beverly and Dereck Joubert

Face to Face with Polar Bears
by Norbert Rosing and Elizabeth Carney

Face to Face with Whales
by Flip and Linda Nicklin

Face to Face with Wolves
by Jim Brandenburg

Oxpecker

Frog

Spider